jewelry
anyone
can make

jewelry anyone can make

Maggi Bennett/ Sarajean Capua/ Jeanette McArthur

Published by Dukane Press, Inc.
Hollywood, Florida

contents

Printed in the United States of America
by Dukane Press, Inc., Hollywood, Florida
Library of Congress Catalog Number: 77-127620
First Edition

ISBN 0-87800-030-5

from the very earliest times, people have adorned themselves with jewelry for decorative purposes and have worn charms and amulets for protective measures against danger and disease.

In ancient Egypt jewelry was important to both men and women. Materials for Egyptian jewelry were gold and occasionally silver and semiprecious stones such as carnelian, red and green jasper, chalcedony, turquoise and lapis lazuli or imitations of these stones made of glass or glazed composition. Techniques known to the ancient craftsmen included cloisonné, granulation, engraving and chasing.

Greek jewelry of the Hellenistic Period was made of gold, encrusted with garnets, amethysts or carnelians and enameled in places. Typical pieces consisted of diadems hung with elaborate pendants, drop earrings, necklaces with pendants on chains and rings set with large stones.

During the Pre-Columbian Period, rich ornaments of metal, semiprecious stones and shells were used by the civilizations from Mexico to Peru. Gold, silver, copper and their alloys were used to make such objects as beads, pendants, nose ornaments and ear disks.

In China jewelry was frequently designed to adorn the costume rather than the person, although hairpins of bone or ivory with the ends carved as birds were popular personal adornment. Other materials used in Chinese jewelry were gilded bronze, silver, amethyst, agate, chalcedony, rose and other colors of quartz and jade.

At the start of the Medieval Period in Europe, the brooch was the most characteristic ornament. Another popular medieval jewel was the devotional pendant, chased or enameled with religious subjects. Cameos were also used throughout the middle ages. In the 14th and 15th centuries, jewelry was fashioned into belts, chaplets, hair nets and necklaces, and sewn on garments.

In modern America jewelry has acquired a streamlined quality and platinum and palladium, because of lightness, have become very popular for gem settings. There has been widespread use of jewelry by men in gem-set signet rings, cuff links and tie tacks or clasps. "Costume" jewelry made of anodized aluminum, silver, plastics, synthetic stones and artificial pearls has become popular. Much of the costume jewelry is finely executed but there are usually thousands of duplicates of each piece so that the person who wants an original one-of-a-kind piece of jewelry must usually pay an exorbitant price or make it himself.

Almost any material from a scrap of cardboard to a piece of silver can be made into a handsome piece of jewelry. This book shows how anyone of any age can make inexpensive jewelry from common materials found around the house or easily purchased in a store. Some of the various examples include jewelry made from wire, yarn, papier mache, cardboard, plaster, rocks and shells. If you like original, unique jewelry that is easy to make, this is the book for you.

cardboard jewelry

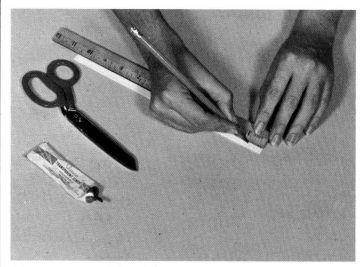

Use one of the types of board called posterboard, railroad board or mat board. (Corrugated cardboard is not satisfactory.) Plan your design, then cut a shape from cardboard. If the jewelry piece is to be a necklace or dangling earrings, pierce the cardboard with an awl or large needle from the front side so the hole will be smooth on the front. Paint the cardboard with tempera or acrylic paint. When dry, coat with clear lacquer or clear plastic spray and your cardboard jewelry will resemble enameled metal. Earring findings may be purchased at handicraft stores and attached with clear cement glue.

Measuring cardboard for square earrings.

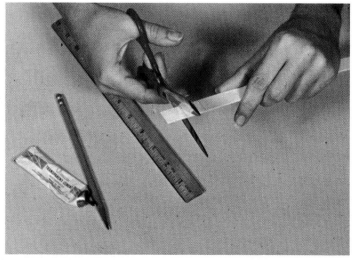

Cutting the cardboard.

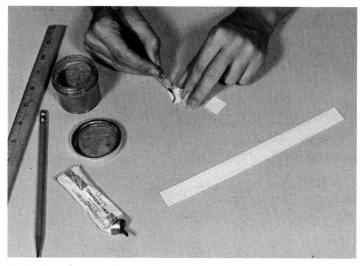

Painting the earrings.

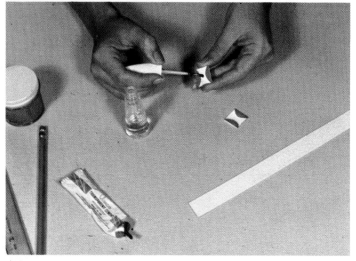

Applying lacquer.

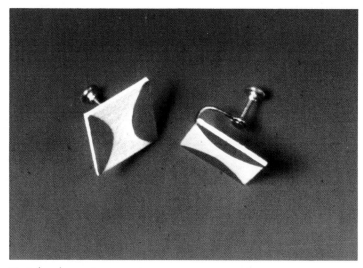

Finished earrings.

The sections of these necklaces were painted with acrylic paint and the designs on the sections were made with small pieces of rug yarn. Identical lengths of yarn were cut and then glued on. When dry, each section was coated with Mache Glaze (a clear finish similar to lacquer, used for coating papier mache projects). Jump rings were used to hold the sections together and a necklace fastener was attached.

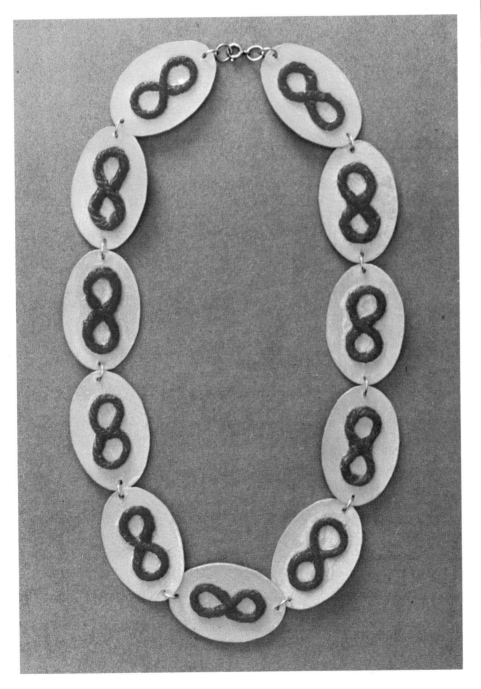

plaster jewelry

Plaster jewelry is easy and inexpensive to make and is lightweight and comfortable to wear. A small amount of Plaster of Paris can be obtained in any hardware store. A box lid makes a satisfactory mold to pour the plaster in. Grease the inside of the box lid with vaseline. Follow the directions on the package for mixing the plaster. A plastic bowl or bucket makes a good container for mixing. When the plaster becomes creamy in consistency, pour it **immediately** into your mold. For most jewelry, ¼ inch thickness is desirable. When the plaster hardens, you may score your slab with a knife for the sizes you wish to make into pins or earrings. Pull the edges of the box lid away from the plaster slab, lift the slab from the box, and break it along the scored lines.

Small rectangles may be smoothed with fine sandpaper on the edges and then have a design painted on with watercolors or tempera paint to make a pin. When the paint is dry and the plaster has thoroughly dried out, coat the design with clear lacquer or clear fingernail polish. Glue a pin back on the back side. Pin backs and other findings are available at handicraft stores.

If you wish, you may carve a free form for pins or earrings or you may cut circles, ovals or any other desired shape. An easy way to obtain a circular shape is to drop small amounts of soft mixed Plaster of Paris from a spoon on a piece of wax paper. If the plaster is soft enough when dropped from the spoon, it will form a circle as it flattens out on the wax paper.

The four rectangular pins in the lower part of the photograph on the opposite page were made by a seven year old child.

button jewelry

Attractive earrings can be made from buttons. Select two that are alike and glue earring backs to the back side or attach ear wires for the pierced ear type. Use a clear cement glue such as Epoxy for gluing. Pendants, cuff links, rings and brooches may also be made from buttons. Felt may be used as a base for a button brooch. If the button is plastic with a protruding piece on the back, this can easily be snipped off with wire cutters or pliers for easier attachment of findings. The ring shown in the picture was made by gluing a button to a ring finding.

jewelry from found objects

Various found objects such as bark, shells, bits of smooth glass, metal and shells can be fashioned into jewelry.

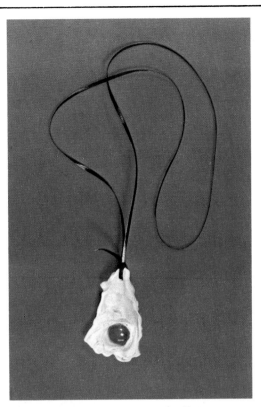

Melted glass on oyster shell

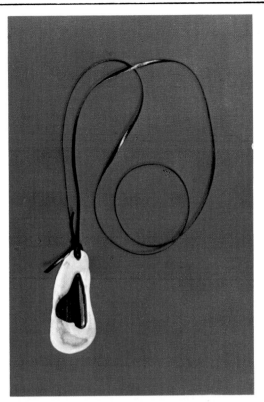

Tiger eye stone on oyster shell

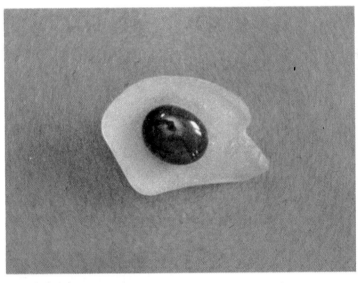

Smooth glass pin

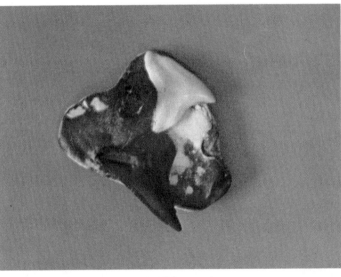

Pin of oyster shell and shark's teeth

Pin of bark and copper

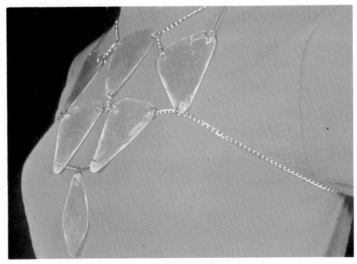

Body chain

craftstrip bracelet

In making a bracelet, you will need 2 strands of craftstrip approximately 3 yards each.

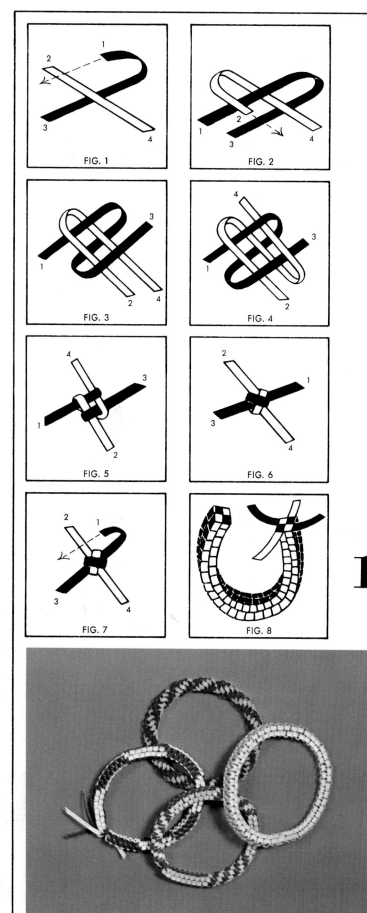

FIG. 1

FIG. 2

FIG. 3

FIG. 4

FIG. 5

FIG. 6

FIG. 7

FIG. 8

1. Arrange the strands as shown in Fig. 1.

2. Take strand 1 across strand 2 leaving a small loop and hold with the thumb and forefinger of the left hand.

3. Fold strand 2 across strands 1 and 3 (Fig. 2).

4. Fold strand 3 across strands 2 and 4 (Fig. 3).

5. Take strand 4 across strand 3 and through the loop left by strand 1 (Fig. 4).

6. Pull all strands to form a square (Fig. 5).

7. Now turn the braid over (upside down as shown in Fig. 6). This is to leave a square at the end of the bracelet.

8. Continue to braid as you started (Fig. 7). Fold strand 1 across strand 2, fold strand 2 across strands 1 and 3, fold strand 3 across strands 2 and 4 and fold strand 4 across strand 3 and through the loop formed by strand 1.

9. Continue the square braid until the bracelet is as large as you want it to be (Fig. 8). Then bring the 2 ends together and interweave the loose ends back into the beginning of the bracelet.

10. When it seems fastened securely, trim excess ends of strands. To make it more secure, a small amount of transparent glue may be inserted into the areas where the ends were trimmed.

For a round bracelet, instead of going back and forth across the square, carry strand 1 **diagonally** across strand 2, carry strand 2 across strands 1 and 3, carry strand 3 across 2 and 4 and insert strand 4 in the loop formed by strand 1. Continuous diagonal braiding will form a round bracelet.

craftstrip over metal

For a two-color craftstrip bracelet, you will need a metal bracelet blank ¾" x 6", two yards of one color craftstrip and three yards of a contrasting color. Cut the two yard piece into seven pieces, ten inches long. Fold 2 inches of each piece over the end of the metal blank and fasten with Scotch tape. Insert the end of the 3 yard piece of craftstrip under the loops at the end of the metal blank. Bind the 7 strips to the blank with three or four turns. Start your design by raising some of the 7 strips and weaving under and over them. Continue the design to within 4 turns of the end of the blank. Bend the seven ends over the end of the metal blank, leaving a small loop in each one. Make the final four turns and put the end of the craftstrip through the loops. Pull the craftstrip tight. Then pull the seven ends tight. Trim all loose ends with sharp scissors or a knife. Bend the bracelet to the desired shape.

A bracelet bender may be made by fastening two ¾" or 1" dowel rods (or ends of broom handles) close together on a piece of wood. Drill holes and insert dowels or nail them from the bottom of the wood. Place the bracelet between the dowel rods and bend it.

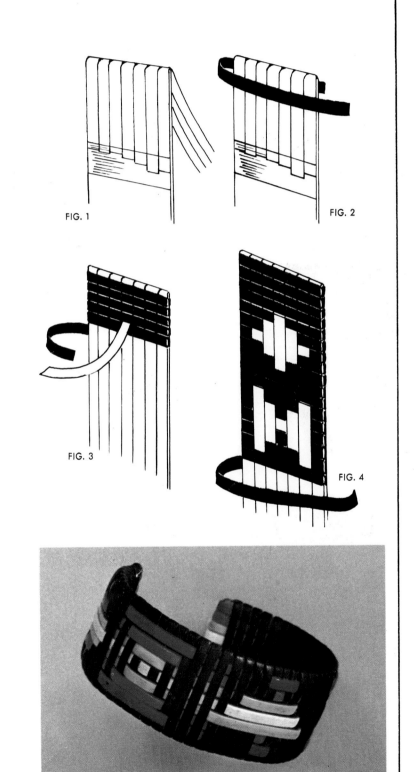

FIG. 1

FIG. 2

FIG. 3

FIG. 4

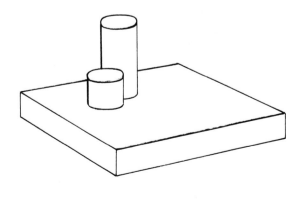

clay jewelry

If you have access to a kiln, ceramic clay may be used to make attractive jewelry, but if no kiln is available, self-hardening clay should be used. When a kiln is used, colored glaze may be used to decorate the clay jewelry. If self-hardening clay is used, the piece may be painted with tempera or other paint and coated with Mache Glaze or clear lacquer.

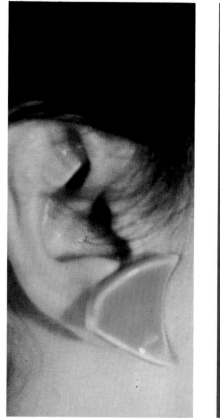

Clay earring fired and glazed.

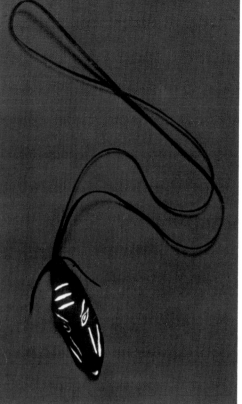

Clay talisman pendant.

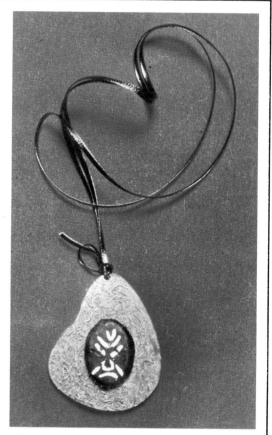

Clay decoration glued to coconut shell.

Indian made clay necklace from Mexico.

Four-leaf clover pendant carved in moist clay, fired and painted.

cookin' crystal jewelry

1. Draw a shape for jewelry on cardboard and cut it out. Take a piece of heavy duty aluminum foil, place the cardboard shape on it and pull the edges of the foil up around the cardboard. Trim the foil with scissors so the sides are approximately ½ inch high.

2. Remove the cardboard shape by inserting a toothpick under it or use tweezers, being careful not to puncture or wrinkle the foil.

3. Sprinkle cookin' crystals evenly into the foil mold. Pat the top smooth. Place the mold with the crystals in an oven which has been preheated to 250° and leave it until the crystals are fused to the desired texture. (½ hour to 1 hour). The longer the crystals are left in the oven, the smoother the texture becomes, however, sometimes a rough or beaded texture is desirable. When the desired texture is obtained, remove the form from the oven and allow it to cool. Remove the foil and glue on the decoration such as polished stone or glass. If the jewelry has been designed for a brooch, finish by gluing on a pin back. If it is to be a pendant, drill a small hole and attach a jump ring and chain. Other items from cookin' crystals might be earrings, cuff links or decorations for key chains.

sequin jewelry

Cut a small shape from felt to use as a base for sewing or gluing your sequins. If you are sewing the sequins, bring your threaded needle from the back side of the felt, through the hole in the sequin and through a small bead, then back through the sequin hole. The bead holds the sequin in place. If you are gluing the sequins, the small beads are not necessary. When you have completed attaching the sequins, you may wish to sew or glue another piece of felt the same size as the original base to the back side. This will reinforce it and make the piece firmer. It will also hide any stitches you have made. Now you are ready to attach the jewelry finding. This may be glued on or sewn.

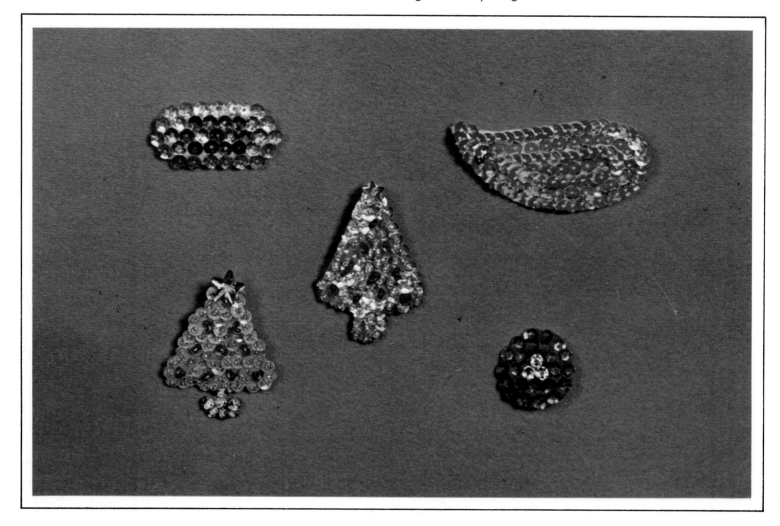

leather jewelry

Scraps of leather or leatherette (vinyl simulated to resemble leather) can be fashioned into attractive items of jewelry. The leaf pin and earring set was made of scraps of yellow and brown top grain cowhide. Scraps were obtained from a furniture upholstering company. Both leaves were wet on the back side and a modeling tool was used to press veins into the leather from the front side. (Any smooth pointed tool such as a nut pick can serve as a modeling tool.) The yellow leaf was tinted with red watercolor to resemble an autumn leaf.

The seal pin was made of black leather. The ball glued to its nose was white leather with alternating sections painted red.

yarn jewelry

1. For a solid color pin, cut a piece of rug yarn about one yard long. Taper the ends by cutting on a slant. Prepare laundry starch. Use instant cold water starch. Make it thick in consistency and remove all lumps.

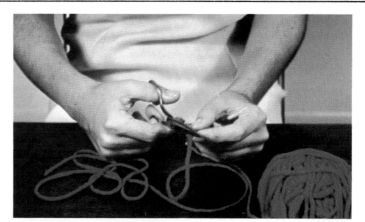

2. Dip the yarn in the starch. As you remove the yarn from the starch, pull it lightly between your fingers to remove excess starch.

3. Place it on wax paper and shape it, starting from the center. If you want more than one color, use the preceding directions but add different colors when desired.

4. As you shape your jewelry, do not pull the yarn too tightly or it will separate as it dries. Push or pat it into place.

5. Allow the piece to dry thoroughly for several days, then remove it from the wax paper and coat it with Mache Glaze or clear lacquer. Attach the proper findings for making a pin, earrings or a necklace.

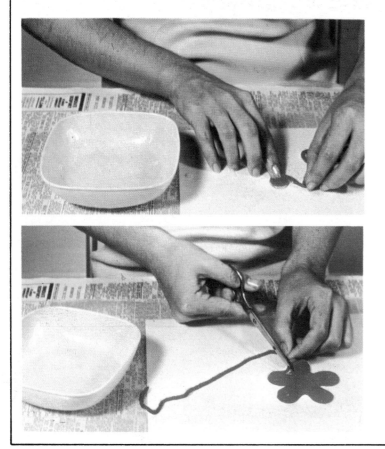

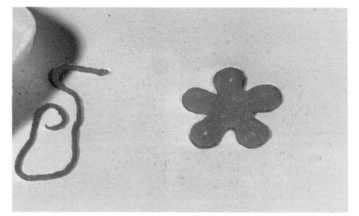

indian bead loom jewelry

Indian bead looms are inexpensive and are available in most handicraft stores. You may make a bead loom by driving ¾ inch wire brads ⅛ inch apart on each end of a piece of wood approximately 2 inches wide by 18 inches long. Using No. 25 linen thread or heavy duty cotton thread, warp the loom by fastening your thread around one of the end nails and carrying it back and forth from one end of the loom to the other. Plan the width of your jewelry and use one more warp thread than the number of beads you want in the width of the jewelry.

1. After warping the bead loom, tie weaving thread near top to outside warp thread. Then string correct number of beads (one less than warp threads) for the first row across.

2. Stretch the weaving thread with the beads on it towards the right UNDER the warp threads. Use your left forefinger to set beads in correct position (one between each of the warp threads). Then bring the weaving thread over the last warp thread and string through all the beads OVER the warp threads.

3. String another group of beads for the second row across. Stretch weaving thread with beads UNDER the warp threads.

4. Bring the weaving thread over the last warp thread and string the needle and weaving thread back through all the beads and OVER the warp threads. Continue until your design is complete.

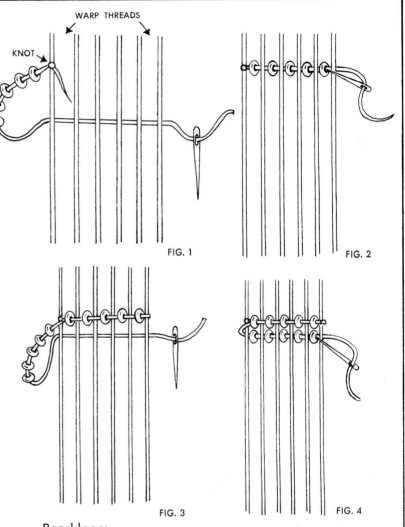

Bead loom

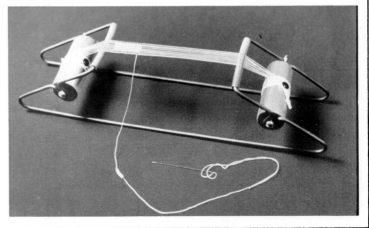

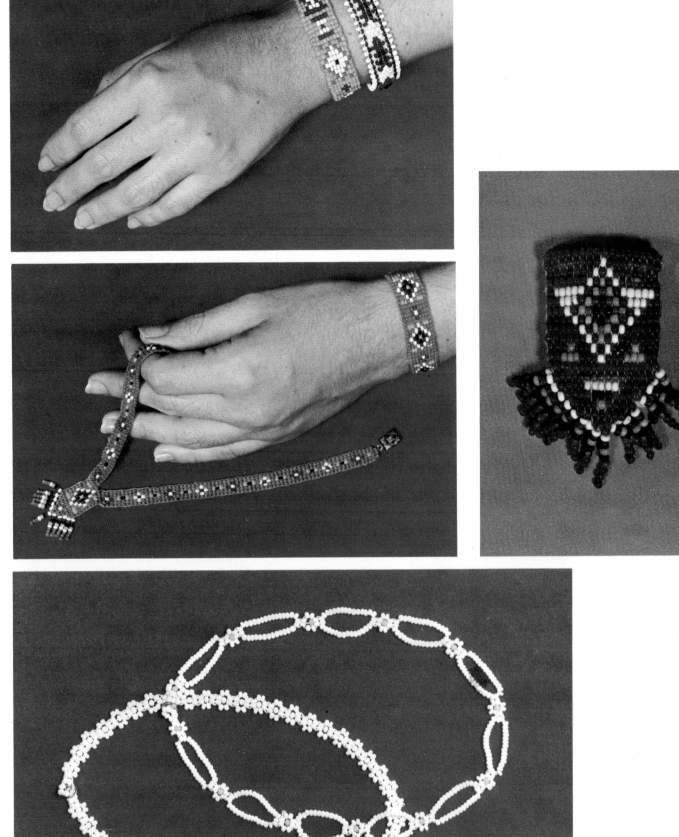

papier mache bracelets

Cut a piece of posterboard the width and length you want for a bracelet. Make the ends meet to form a circle. On the top side, put a piece of masking tape to hold the ends together. **Do not overlap the ends** as this would make the bracelet rough inside. Make a papier mache mixture by tearing facial or toilet tissue into small pieces and adding water and paste (either soft white paste or wheat paste) until the mixture is pliable.

A commercial papier mache called Celluclay is available in most handicraft stores. Celluclay does not require any paste. You simply add water and stir it and it is immediately ready for use.

Begin to put papier mache on the outside of your bracelet form. Press it down toward the edges for a rounded effect. The yellow and orange bracelets in the photograph were formed in this manner. If you wish to make your bracelet of uniform flatness on top, roll your papier mache mixture on wax paper with a rolling pin covered with wax paper also. (Celluclay works well for this method.) Cut a piece from this slab the exact width and length of your bracelet form and put it on the top side. The green and blue bracelets in the photograph were made by this method.

If you wish to decorate your bracelet, wait until the Celluclay or papier mache has dried, then squeeze Elmer's or similar glue into a design or glue on pieces of twine and paint when dry. If you want small stones on your bracelet, they can be glued on after the bracelet has been painted. Suitable paints are tempera or acrylics. If tempera is used, it should be coated with clear lacquer or Mache Glaze to preserve it.

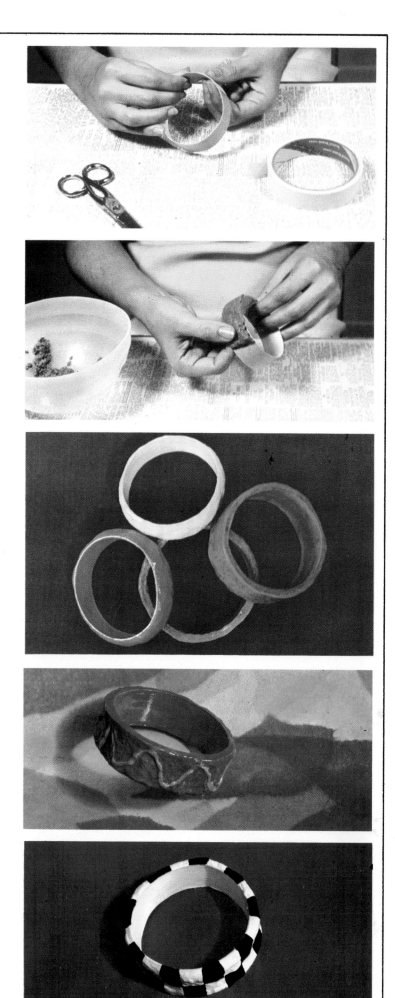

papier mache pins

Using soft white paste, put together about six or seven layers of paper about the size you want your jewelry to be. The paper may be newspaper, typing paper, newsprint or paper of similar thickness. The top and bottom layer should be unlined and unprinted paper. Be sure to completely cover each layer with paste and smooth out any wrinkles. When all layers have been pasted together, before it has time to harden, cut out your desired shape. It is helpful to have a design made previously. While the form is still soft and damp with the paste, it may be bent and shaped. Small scraps from the original layered piece may be pasted on to create a raised design or shapes of papier mache may be added. When dry, paint with tempera and coat with clear lacquer or use acrylic paint.

A stone or piece of glass may be added for decoration.

Attach a pin back to complete your piece of jewelry.

Pendants and earrings may be made by this method.

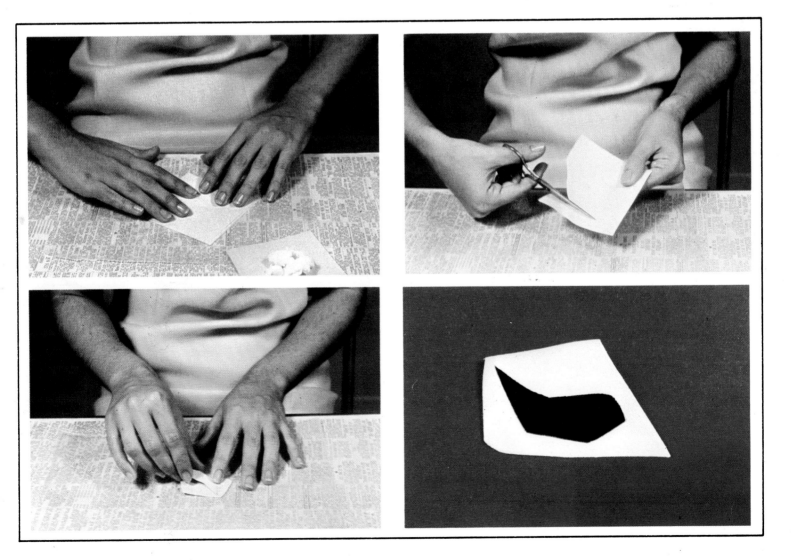

Papier Mache Jewelry

aluminum foil jewelry

1. Make a form for the jewelry. If you are making a bracelet, a papier mache form makes a good base. (See page 20 for papier mache.) You may use an old bracelet for the base. Thin white glue with water (about 1 part water to 3 parts glue). Crinkle aluminum foil and then straighten it out again.

2. Brush the glue mixture on the bracelet form and cover it with the crinkled foil, shiny side up.

3. Smooth the edges together inside the bracelet so there will not be any rough edges. Let it dry overnight.

4. Spray the bracelet with flat black paint and wipe it immediately with a soft cloth. This will give the appearance of hand hammered silver. When the paint is dry, spray the bracelet with clear acrylic fixative to make the finish more permanent.

These pins were made by the same method. One had a piece of cord and the other a cardboard fish shape glued to the base to make a raised design.

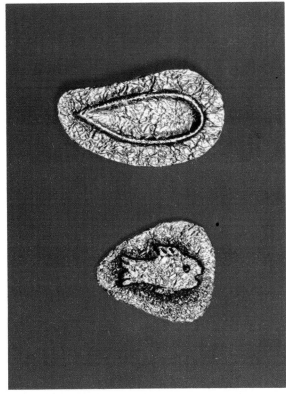

simulated silver jewelry

Expensive looking simulated silver jewelry may be created from an assortment of inexpensive materials which include tagboard, Sculp-Metal and Rub 'n Buff.

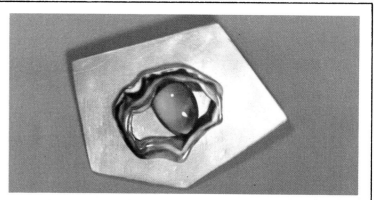

Sculp-Metal pin with agate and melted glass

1. Design a form on the tagboard in pencil. The finished product will appear more distinctive if another smaller shape is designed to give depth to the piece. This additional form may best be adhered to the original shape with rubber cement.

Cutting shape

2. Thin a small amount of Sculp-Metal in a jar with Sculp-Metal Thinner. Brush some of the solution over the tagboard with a small brush or popsicle stick, taking care to coat the entire surface evenly and rapidly, and for best results, do not touch the brush or stick twice in the same spot as the Sculp-Metal dries very fast. At least four coats should be applied to front, sides and back. Wait several minutes between each application.

Adding shape

3. After the final coating, notice whether there is any indication of curling sides. If curling is observed, shape the sides gently and allow to harden thoroughly for several hours.

Applying Sculp-Metal

Completing application of Sculp-Metal

Rubbing with steel wool.

Rubbing with ebony Rub 'n Buff.

Rubbing with silver Rub 'n Buff.

Completed pin.

4. When dry, smooth the surface gently with a fine grade of steel wool. Then rub black stove polish or ebony Rub 'n Buff on the areas where accent is desired. Apply silver leaf Rub 'n Buff to the remaining surface with a soft cloth. When rubbed sparingly, the appearance of antique hand-hammered silver is given.

5. Allow to dry for a few minutes, then polish to the desired patina. If it is preferred, copper or gold leaf Rub 'n Buff may be substituted for the silver leaf. Upon adding the necessary finding, the creation of a seemingly expensive artifice is complete.

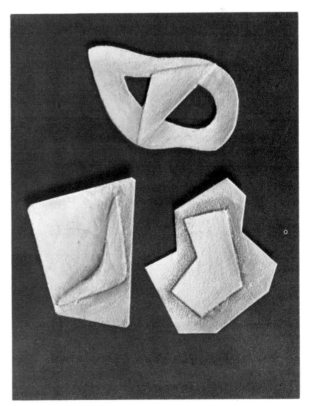

Other Sculp-Metal pins.

wire jewelry

Copper or aluminum wire, about 20 gauge, is easy to bend into various designs.

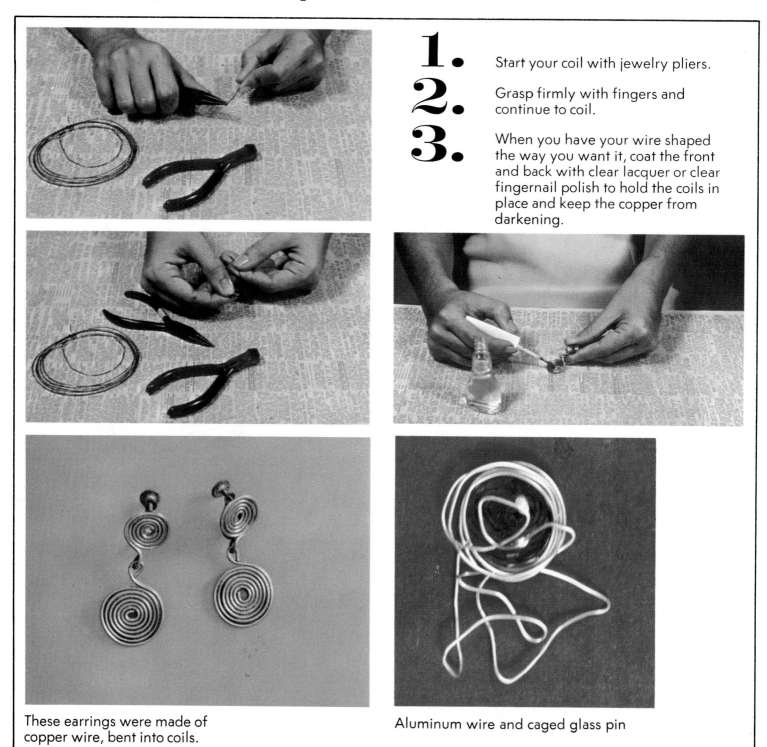

1. Start your coil with jewelry pliers.

2. Grasp firmly with fingers and continue to coil.

3. When you have your wire shaped the way you want it, coat the front and back with clear lacquer or clear fingernail polish to hold the coils in place and keep the copper from darkening.

These earrings were made of copper wire, bent into coils.

Aluminum wire and caged glass pin

aluminum jewelry

Aluminum jewelry resembles silver jewelry but is easier to make, doesn't tarnish and is less expensive. Strips of aluminum in gauge 22 are available at most handicraft stores. In making metal jewelry, you will need jewelry shears or small metal snips.

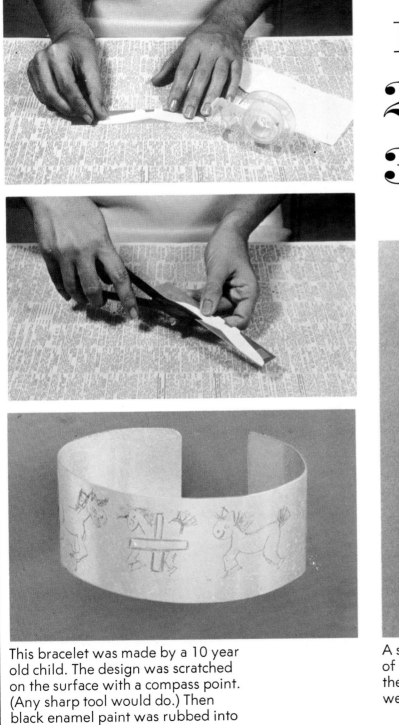

1. Make a design on paper and tape it on a piece of aluminum.

2. Use jewelry shears to cut the design from aluminum.

3. Buff the aluminum if a buffer is available. If not, rub it with fine steel wool (000) or (0000).

This bracelet was made by a 10 year old child. The design was scratched on the surface with a compass point. (Any sharp tool would do.) Then black enamel paint was rubbed into the incised design.

A small hole was drilled in each end of this aluminum pendant to attach the chain and the polished stones were glued on.

copper jewelry

In making copper jewelry, you will need pieces of copper from about gauge 18 to gauge 22. If it is thinner than gauge 22, it may bend too easily and not hold its shape very well. If it is heavier than gauge 18, it will be difficult to cut and shape.

This copper flower pin was made by cutting two shapes of five petals and overlapping them so that 10 petals are showing. The petals were bent slightly forward and the top section was soldered to the bottom section. A small soldering gun was used for this. However, liquid solder could have been used or even a cement glue. The center was a small circle of copper, dented by tapping it with a nail and hammer. Copper wire was used for the stem and veins in the leaves. These were soldered in place and a pin back was soldered to the back of the flower.

This pin was made with a shape of copper for the background, a piece of copper wire curved around a piece of copper screen in the center and two small scraps of copper attached for additional decoration.

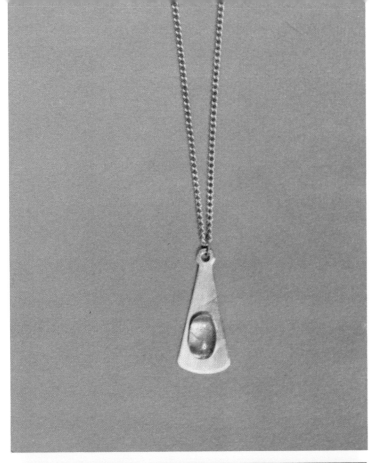

This pendant was made of copper and a small piece of melted glass was glued on.

The background for this pendant was a piece of copper. A cross was cut from aluminum and attached with liquid solder. A hole was drilled in the top of the copper, and a jump ring was inserted to hold the chain.

silver jewelry

Silver is sometimes difficult to find, however some handicraft stores carry circles approximately one inch, one and one-half inches and two inches in diameter, narrow silver strips and silver wire, which may be purchased by the inch or foot.

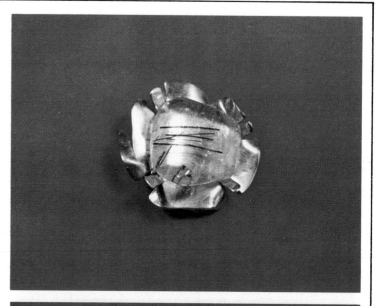

This pin was made from a silver circle 1½ inches in diameter. Jewelry shears were used to slit the edges. Then they were filed to smooth and round them. A piece of crystal quartz with tourmaline was glued to the center with epoxy glue and a pin back was attached to complete the piece.

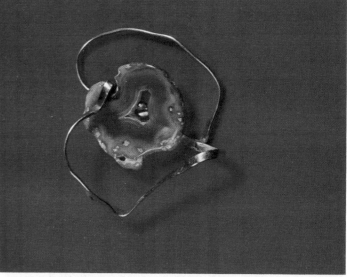

A narrow strip of silver was bent and shaped around a piece of agate with a small garnet in the center. One end of the silver strip was secured to the back of the agate and the other end to another section of the silver strip. A pin back completed this jewelry.

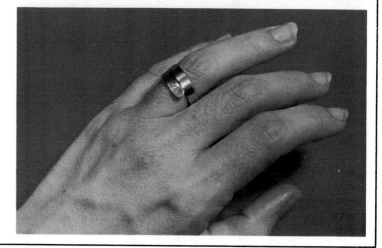

This ring was made from a strip of silver. The ends were filed round and curved to pass each other. A ring of this type requires no stone or soldering. It is also adjustable to different sizes. A sharp tool such as a scribe, a steel needle or compass point can be used to inscribe initials or other designs into the silver.

silver wire jewelry

This necklace was made from silver wire bent into a circle. An extra piece of wire was soldered to the lower part of the circle and curved with a small loop at the end. A jump ring was inserted and attached to a bell cap glued to a piece of agate. The top ends of the circle of wire were bent into small loops and the ends soldered. A necklace fastener was attached with a jump ring.

index

Other Dukane Craft/Art books by the authors:

Stitchery — 010

Creative Crayon Techniques — 028

Printing Without a Press — 029

Holiday Ideas — 031

Ends & Odds to Art — 032

DUKANE PRESS
HOLLYWOOD, FLA.